How Happiness Happens

UNEXPECTED CONTENTMENT

You Don't Have To Search Very Far For It

COLIN SANDOVAL

Table of Contents

Chapter 1: Live A Long, Important Life 6
Chapter 2: Meditate For Focus 9
Chapter 3: Things That Spark Joy 12
Chapter 4: How To Stop Lying To Ourselves: A Call For Self-Awareness 15
Chapter 5: *Never Stop Even If Someone Tells You To* 18
Chapter 6: *Motivation With Good Feelings* 20
Chapter 7: How To Find Motivation 23
Chapter 8: Happy People Stay Present 29
Chapter 9: Nothing Is Impossible 31
Chapter 10: Trust The Process 34
Chapter 11: Keep Moving When Things Get Hard 36
Chapter 12: How To Use Military Strategy To Build Better Habits 40
Chapter 13: The Struggle With Time 45
Chapter 14: How to Value Being Alone 48
Chapter 15: If You Commit to Nothing, You'll Be Distracted By Everything 51
Chapter 16: How To Stick To Your Goals When Life Gets Crazy 54
Chapter 17: How To Find Your Passion 58
Chapter 18: How To Simplify Your Life And Maximise Your Results 62
Chapter 19: Motivate Yourself 64
Chapter 20: How To Focus and Concentrate On Your Work 67
Chapter 21: **Happy People Take Care of Themselves** 71
Chapter 22: Happy People Surround Themselves with The Right People 74
Chapter 23: It's Not Your Job to Tell Yourself "No" 77
Chapter 24: Happy People Use Their Character Strengths 80
Chapter 25: *How to Stop Chasing New Goals All the Time* 83

Chapter 26: Happy People View Problems as Challenges 86
Chapter 27: It's Okay To Feel Uncertain 89
Chapter 28: Consistency 92
Chapter 29: *Happy People Stay Grateful For Everything They Have* 95
Chapter 30: Being Open To Opportunities For Social Events 97
Chapter 31: Being Mentally Strong 101
Chapter 32: The Trick To Focusing 103
Chapter 33: The Things That Matter 106
Chapter 34: *Keep Working When You're Just Not Feeling It* 111
Chapter 35: HOW TO DEVELOP AN INCREDIBLE WORK ETHIC 114
Chapter 36: 10 Stress Management Tips 117

Chapter 1:
Live A Long, Important Life

Do you think you are more capable to deal with the failure or the regret of not trying at all?

Are you living the life you want or the life everyone else wants for you?

Would you feel good spending your time on entertainment that might not last for long? Or would you feel good feeling like you are growing and have a better self of you to look at in the mirror?

Similarly, would like to live in the present or would you love to work for a better future?

Do you want money to dictate your life or do you want money to follow you where ever you go?

Would you prefer being tired or being broke?

Do you want to spend the rest of your life in this place where you and your parents were born? Or do you won't go around the world and find new possibilities in even the most remote places?

Would you rather risk it all or play it safe?

We are often presented with all these questions in our lifetime. Most people take these questions as a way to enter into your adulthood. The answers to these questions are meant to show you the actual meaning of life.

So what is Life? Life is not your parents, your work, your friends, your events, and your functions. It's within you and around you.

You should learn to live your life to the fullest. You should love to live your life for as long as you can with a happy body and a healthy mind.

A happy and healthy body and mind are important. Because you can only feel secure on a stable platform. You can only wish to stand on a platform where you know you can stay put for a long time.

There is nothing wrong with working eight or nine hours in your daily life. It's not unhealthy or anything. Working is what gives our life a purpose. Working is what keeps us active, moving, and motivated.

We have one life, and we have to make it matter. But the way we chose to do it is what matters the most. Our choices make us who we are rather than our actions.

The life we live is the epitome of our intentions and morals. We can be defined in a single word or a single phrase if we ever try. We don't need to analyze someone else, we just need to see ourselves in the mirror and we might be able to see right across the image.

The day we are able to do that, might be the day we have actually made a worthy human being of ourselves and have fulfilled our destiny.

If you are able to look at yourself and go through your whole life in the blink of an eye and cherish the memories as if you were right there at that moment. Believe me, you have had a long and important life to make you think of it all over again every day.

Chapter 2:
Meditate For Focus

Meditation calms the mind and helps you to focus on what is important. It dims the noise and brings your goals into clearer vision.

Meditation has been practised as far back as 5000bc in India - with meditation depicted in wall artisan from that period.
That is 1500 years older than any written artefact ever found.
It is as old as the archaeological evidence of any human society.

Meditation can change the structure of the brain promoting focus, learning and better memory, as well as lowering stress and reducing the chances of anxiety and depression.

Whilst there are many different types and ways to meditate,
the ultimate goal is to clear your mind and calm your body
so that you can focus on your dream.
Aim to look inward for answers.
It could be aided by music relating to your dream or videos.
The music, the images, and imagining you are already living that life will bring it into reality.

Your mind creates the vision and the feeling
in your heart will bring it to you.

When your mind and heart work together it creates balance,
leading to happiness and success.

Meditation is the process of bringing the
visions of the mind and the desires of the heart together,
which in turn will form your life.
Meditation clears all the threats to this -
such as worry and distraction.
It will bring you clear focus and open up the next steps in your journey.

Meditation is often best done when you first wake or before you go to sleep, but it can be incorporated into your day.
If clear consistent thought brings decisive action and success,
it is important to dwell on your dreams as often as possible.
Calm your mind of the unnecessary noise that is robbing you of your focus.

The more realistic you make this vision
and the more you feel it in your heart,
the quicker it will come.

Meditation can help you achieve this
whether you follow a guide or make it up yourself.
The key is calm and focus.

Your subconscious knows how to get there.
Meditation will help open up that knowledge.

Science is just beginning to unlock the answers on why meditation is so effective, even so it has been used for over 7000 years to help people relax and focus on their goals.

The positive health and well-being evidence of meditation is well documented.
We may not yet understand it fully,
But just know that it works and use it every day.
You don't need to understand every detail to use something that works.
Meditation is perhaps one of the most time tested tools in existence.
It could work for you, if you try it.
It could change your life forever.

Chapter 3:
Things That Spark Joy

I'm sure you've heard the term "spark joy", and this is our topic of discussion today that I am going to borrow heavily from Marie Kondo.

Now why do I find the term spark joy so fascinating and why have i used it extensively in all areas of my life ever since coming across that term a few years ago?

When I first watched Marie Kondo's show on Netflix and also reading articles on how this simple concept that she has created has helped people declutter their homes by choosing the items that bring joy to them and discarding or giving away the ones that don't, I began my own process of decluttering my house of junk from clothes to props to ornaments, and even to furniture.

I realised that many things that looked good or are the most aesthetically pleasing, aren't always the most comfortable to use or wear. And when they are not my go to choice, they tend to sit on shelves collecting dust and taking up precious space in my house. And after going through my things one by one, this recurring theme kept propping up time and again. And i subconsciously associated comfort and ease of use with things that spark joy to me. If I could pick something up easily without hesitation to use or wear, they tend to me things that I gravitated to naturally, and these things began to spark joy when i used them. And when i started getting rid of things that I don't find particularly pleased to use, i felt my house was only filled with enjoyable things that I not only enjoyed looking at, but also using on a regular and frequent basis.

This association of comfort and ease of use became my life philosophy. It didn't apply to simply just decluttering my home, but also applied to the process of acquiring in the form of shopping. Every time i would pick something up and consider if it was worthy of a purpose, i would examine whether this thing would be something that I felt was comfortable and that i could see myself utilising, and if that answer was no, i would put them down and never consider them again because i knew deep down that it would not spark joy in me as I have associated joy with comfort.

This simple philosophy has helped saved me thousands of dollars in frivolous spending that was a trademark of my old self. I would buy things on the fly without much consideration and most often they would end up as white elephants in my closet or cupboard.

To me, things that spark joy can apply to work, friends, and relationships as well. Expanding on the act of decluttering put forth by Marie Kondo. If the things you do, and the people you hang out with don't spark you much joy, then why bother? You would be better off spending time doing things with people that you actually find fun and not waste everybody's time in the process. I believe you would also come out of it being a much happier person rather than forcing yourself to be around people and situations that bring you grief.

Now that is not to say that you shouldn't challenge yourself and put yourself out there. But rather it is to give you a chance to assess the things you do around you and to train yourself to do things that really spark joy in you that it becomes second nature. It is like being fine tuned to your 6th sense in a way because ultimately we all know what we truly like and dislike, however we choose to ignore these feelings and that costs us time effort and money.

So today's challenge is for you to take a look at your life, your home, your friendships, career, and your relationships. Ask yourself, does this thing spark joy? If it doesn't, maybe you should consider a decluttering of sorts from all these different areas in your life and to streamline it to a more minimalist one that you can be proud of owning each and every piece.

Chapter 4: How To Stop Lying To Ourselves: A Call For Self-Awareness

If you're serious about getting better at something, then one of the first steps is to know—in black-and-white terms—where you stand. You need self-awareness before you can achieve self-improvement.

Here are some tools I use to make myself more self-aware:

WORKOUT JOURNAL

For the past five years, I have used my workout journal to record each workout I do. While it can be interesting to leaf back through old workouts and see the progress I've made, I have found this method to be most useful every week. When I go to the gym next week, I will look at the weights I lifted the week before and try to make a small increase. It's so simple, but the workout journal helps me avoid wasting time in the gym, wandering around, and just "doing some stuff." With this basic tracking, I can make focused improvements each week.

ANNUAL REVIEWS AND INTEGRITY REPORTS

At the end of each year, I conduct my Annual Review, where I summarize the progress I've made in business, health, travel, and other areas. I also take time each spring to do an Integrity Report where I challenge myself to provide proof of how I am living by my core values. These two practices give me a chance to track and measure the "softer" areas of my life. It can be difficult to know for certain if you're doing a better job of living by your values, but these reports at least force me to track these issues on a consistent basis.

A CALL FOR SELF-AWARENESS

If you aren't aware of what you're actually doing, then it is very hard to change your life with any degree of consistency. Trying to build better habits without self-awareness is like firing arrows into the night. You can't expect to hit the bullseye if you're not sure where the target is located.

Furthermore, I have discovered very few people who naturally do the right thing without ever measuring their behavior. For example, I know a handful of people who maintain six-pack abs without worrying too much about what they eat. However, every single one of them weighed and measured their food at some point. After months of counting calories and measuring their meals, they developed the ability to judge their meals appropriately.

In other words, measurement brought their levels of self-awareness in line with reality. You can wing it *after* you measure it. Once you're aware of what's actually going on, you can make accurate decisions based on "gut-feel" because your gut is based on something accurate.

In short, start by measuring something.

Chapter 5:
Never Stop Even If Someone Tells You To

Your brain works in mysterious ways, and it has a way of complying with negative things much faster than the positives. It is a part of human nature to not accept things that make one feel good about themselves because if they do, they are termed "narcissistic" or "self-obsessed."

With the way things have taken a turn, the world has become a much more competitive place, and one needs to shoot for the moon to land among the stars. In a world so fast, if you can come up with unique and different ideas from others, not only do you stand out, but it also gives rise to the opposition. This is where people start discouraging you and telling you how you are not good enough. This is where your idea gets lost in their judgment, and you start doubting yourself and question if everything is worth it or not.

A million people out there are ready to step on you and crush your self-esteem and confidence because that is what they strive for. If you give them the strength and ability to take that away from you, it is in your hands. One of the strongest weapons one has is self-confidence which can take them to places they had only dreamt of, but if it is crushed, all that is ahead is failure and insecurities. As Johann Wolfgang von Goethe said, "As soon as you trust yourself, you will know how to live."

The path of success is never doubting yourself when someone tells you "No" and moving forward by trusting yourself instead of putting it in their judgment. If people's opinions measured success, great people like Albert Einstein wouldn't have made history. He failed school at the age of 16 and was told that he would always be a failure but imagine if he had stopped then, who would have developed the theory of relativity? Probably no one!

The truth is that while you might be good in one thing, you will always lack in one thing or another and you will be made felt like you are a failure. It is important not to listen to people when they tell you to stop because you cannot do it. You can! And you should not believe otherwise. Imagine if Einstein was asked to write a love song? Or Rihanna to come up with a theory of relativity? We wouldn't have had a world-class singer or a physicist. Thus, it is important to figure out your strengths and work towards polishing them. Move on with things and put in that belief that you can do it. Because trust us, if you tell yourself, you can do it. No one telling you otherwise will matter!

Chapter 6:
<u>Motivation With Good Feelings</u>

Ever wonder what goes on in your mind when you feel depressed isn't always the reaction to the things that happen to you? What you go through when you feel down is the chemistry of your brain that you yourself allow being created in the first place.

You don't feel weak just because your heart feels so heavy. You feel weak because you have filled your heart with all these feelings that don't let you do something useful.

Feelings are not your enemy till you choose the wrong ones. In fact, Feelings and emotions can be the strongest weapon to have in your arsenal.

People say, "You are a man, so act like one. Men don't cry, they act strong and brave"

You must make yourself strong enough to overcome any feelings of failure or fear. Any thought that makes you go aloof and dims that light of creativity and confidence. It's OK to feel sad and cry for some time, but it's not OK to feel weak for even a second.

Your consciousness dictates your feelings. Your senses help you to process a moment and in turn help you translate them into feelings that go both ways. This process has been going on from the day you were born and will continue till your last day.

You enter your consciousness as soon as you open your eyes to greet the day. It is at this moment when your creativity is at its peak. What you need now is just a set of useful thoughts and emotions that steer your whole day into a worthwhile one.

Don't spend your day regretting and repressing things you did or someone else did to you. You don't need these feelings right now. Because you successfully passed those tests of life and are alive still to be grateful for what you have right now.

There are a billion things in life to be thankful for and a billion more to be sad for. But you cannot live a happy fulfilling life if you focus on the later ones.

Life is too short to be sad and to be weak. When you start your day, don't worry about what needs to be done. But think about who you need to be to get those things done.
Don't let actions and outcomes drive you. Be the sailor of yourself to decide what outcomes you want.

Believe me, the feeling of gratitude is the biggest motivator. Self gratitude should be the level of appraisal to expect. Nothing should matter after your own opinions about yourself.

If you let other people's opinions affect your feelings, you are the weakest person out there. And failure is your destination.

Visualization of a better life can help you feel and hope better. It would help you to grow stronger and faster but remember; The day you lose control of your emotions, feelings, and your temper, your imagination will only lead you to a downward spiral.

Chapter 7:
How To Find Motivation

Today we're going to talk about a topic that hopefully will help you find the strength and energy to do the work that you've told yourself you've wanted or needed to but always struggle to find the one thing that enables you to get started and keep going. We are going to help you find motivation.

In this video, I am going to break down the type of tasks that require motivation into 2 distinct categories. Health and fitness, and work. As I believe that these are the areas where most of you struggle to stay motivated. With regards to family, relationships, and other areas, i dont think motivation is a real problem there.

For all of you who are struggling to motivate yourself to do things you've been putting off, for example getting fit, going to the gym, motivation to stay on a diet, to keep working hard on that project, to study for your exams, to do the chores, or to keep working on your dreams... All these difficult things require a huge amount of energy from us day in and day out to be consistent and to do the work.

I know... it can be incredibly difficult. Having experienced these ups and downs in my own struggle with motivation, it always starts off swimmingly... When we set a new year's resolution, it is always easy to think that we will stick to our goal in the beginning. We are super motivated to go do the gym to lose those pounds, and we go every single day for about a week... only to give up shortly after because we either don't see results, or we just find it too difficult to keep up with the regime.

Same goes for starting a new diet... We commit to doing these things for about a week, but realize that we just simply don't like the process and we give up as well...

Finding motivation to study for an important exam or working hard on work projects are a different kind of animal. As these are things that have a deadline. A sense of urgency that if we do not achieve our desired result, we might fail or get fired from our company. With these types of tasks, most of us are driven by fear, and fear becomes our motivator... which is also not healthy for us as stress hormones builds within us as we operate that way, and we our health pays for it.

Let's start with tackling the first set of tasks that requires motivation. And i would classify this at the health and fitness level. Dieting, exercise, going to the gym, eating healthily, paying attention to your sleep... All these things are very important, but not necessarily urgent to many of us. The deadline we set for ourselves to achieve these health goals are arbitrary. Based on the images we see of models, or people who seem pretty fit around us, we set an unrealistic deadline for ourselves to achieve those body goals. But more often than not, body changes don't happen in days or weeks for most of us by the way we train. It could take up to months or years... For those celebrities and fitness models you see on Instagram or movies, they train almost all day by personal trainers. And their deadline is to look good by the start of shooting for the movie. For most of us who have day jobs, or don't train as hard, it is unrealistic to expect we can achieve that body in the same amount of time. If we only set aside 1 hour a day to exercise, while we may get gradually fitter, we shouldn't expect that amazing transformation to happen so quickly. It is why so many of us set ourselves up for failure.

To truly be motivated to keep to your health and fitness goals, we need to first define the reasons WHY we even want to achieve these results in the first place. Is it to prove to yourself that you have discipline? Is it to look good for your wedding photoshoot? Is it for long term health and fitness? Is it so that you don't end up like your relatives who passed too soon because of their poor health choices? Is it to make yourself more attractive so that you can find a man or woman in your life? Or is it just so that you can live a long and healthy life, free of medical complications that plague most seniors by the time they hit their 60s and 70s? What are YOUR reasons WHY you want to keep fit? Only after you know these reasons, will you be able to truly set a realistic deadline for your health goals. For those that are in it for a better health overall until their ripe old age, you will realize that this health goal is a life long thing. That you need to treat it as a journey that will take years and decades. And small changes each day will add up. Your motivator is not to go to the gym 10 hours a day for a week, but to eat healthily consistently and exercise regularly every single day so that you will still look and feel good 10, 20, 30, 50 years, down the road.

And for those that need an additional boost to motivate you to keep the course, I want you to find an accountability partner. A friend that will keep you in check. And hopefully a friend that also has the same health and fitness goals as you do. Having this person will help remind you not to let yourself and this person down. Their presence will hopefully motivate you to not let your guard down, and their honesty in pointing out that you've been slacking will keep you in check constantly that you will do as you say.

And if you still require an additional boost on top of that, I suggest you print and paste a photo of the body that you want to achieve and the idol that you wish to emulate in terms of having a good health and fitness on a board where you can see every single day. And write down your reasons why beside it. That way, you will be motivated everytime you walk past this board to keep to your goals always.

Now lets move on to study and work related tasks. For those with a fixed 9-5 job and deadlines for projects and school related work, your primary motivator right now is fear. Which as we established earlier, is not exactly healthy. What we want to do now is to change these into more positive motivators. Instead of thinking of the consequences of not doing the task, think of the rewards you would get if you completed it early. Think of the relief you will feel knowing that you had not put off the work until the last minute. And think of the benefits that you will gain... less stress, more time for play, more time with your family, less worry that you have to cram all the work at the last possible minute, and think of the good results you will get, the opportunities that you will have seized, not feeling guilty about procrastinations... and any other good stuff that you can think of. You could also reward yourself with a treat or two for completing the task early. For example buying your favourite food, dessert, or even gadgets. All these will be positive motivators that will help you get the ball moving quicker so that you can get to those rewards sooner. Because who likes to wait to have fun anyway?

Now I will move on to talk to those who maybe do not have a deadline set by a boss or teacher, but have decided to embark on a new journey by themselves. Whether it be starting a new business, getting your accounting done, starting a new part time venture.. For many of these tasks, the only motivator is yourself. There is no one breathing down your neck to get the job done fast and that could be a problem in itself. What should we do in that situation? I believe with this, it is similar to how we motivate ourselves in the heath and fitness goals. You see, sheer force doesn't always work sometimes. We need to establish the reasons why we want to get all these things done early in life. Would it be to fulfil a dream that we always had since we were a kid? Would it be to earn an extra side income to travel the world? Would it be to prove to yourself that you can have multiple streams of income? Would it to become an accomplished professional in a new field? Only you can define your reasons WHY you want to even begin and stay on this new path in the first place. So only you can determine why and how you can stay on the course to eventually achieve it in the end.

Similarly for those of you who need additional help, I would highly recommend you to get an accountability partner. Find someone who is in similar shoes as you are, whether you are an entrepreneur, or self-employed, or freelance, find someone who can keep you in check, who knows exactly what you are going through, and you can be each other's pillars of support when one of you finds yourself down and out. Or needs a little pick me up. There is a strong motivator there for you to keep you on course during the rough time.

And similar to health and fitness goal, find an image on the web that resonates with the goal you are trying to achieve. Whether it might be to buy a new house, or to become successful, i want that image to always be available to you to look at every single day. That you never forget WHY you began the journey. This constant reminder should light a fire in you each and everyday to get you out of your mental block and to motivate you to take action consistently every single day.

So I challenge each and every one of you to find motivation in your own unique way. Every one of you have a different story to tell, are on different paths, and no two motivators for a person are the same. Go find that one thing that would ignite a fire on your bottom everytime you look at it. Never forget the dream and keep staying the course until you reach the summit.

Chapter 8:
Happy People Stay Present

"Realize deeply that the present moment is all you ever have."

According to a study, 50% of the time, we are not fully present in the moment. We are either thinking about the past or worrying about the future. These things lead to frustration, anxiety, and pain in our daily life. Each morning as soon as we wake up, we start seeking distractions. As we wake up with a clear mind, we should be grateful for a new day that we got; instead, we start looking for our phone, start going through interwebs and rush into our days. So now we are going to help you and list some of the things that will help you stay present.

Stop Being a Slave to Your Mind: For the next four days, let's do an exercise where you pay attention to your thoughts and see what crosses your mind. You. You will soon realize that majority of the thoughts that you have are destructive. There will be very little time to think about the present, and the majority of your thoughts would be about the past or the future. So, whenever this happens and you find yourself wandering consciously, try to bring yourself back to the present. Also, you need to remind yourself that multi-tasking is a myth and focus on one thing only.

Tap into Your Senses: If you mindfully tap into your senses, you will realize that it is a fantastic way of bringing more awareness into your day. Because our eyes are wide open all day, we can see, but we forget to tap into other senses such as taste, touch, or smell. But if you use these, you can feel more present and calm down if you are in a stressful situation. You might not realize this, but our senses play a huge role in manifesting our reality. For example, everything we are hearing we are touching will regularly turn into our reality. That is why we can use the power our senses have and feel more calm and present.

Listen Closely: Everyone loves to talk, but only a few people like to listen. People love to share their dreams, what they have accomplished and what they desire, and still, nobody seems to be listening closely.

"When you talk, you are only repeating what you already know. But if you listen, you may learn something new."

When you listen carefully, you will be able to charm people and at the same time learn new things and be present. Because you will be focusing on what they are saying, you will focus on the current moment. This way, you will also be able to silence your thoughts about the past and future because you will be consciously listening and focusing on what they are saying. This will also benefit your relationship in the long run because when you need an ear to listen to your problems, they will be there for you. This is a win-win situation for you, and you will improve your relationship while practising being more present.

Chapter 9:
Nothing Is Impossible

Success is a concept as individual as beauty is, in the eye of the beholder, but with each individuals success comes testing circumstances, the price that must be paid in advance.

The grind,

The pain and the losses all champions have endured.

These hardships are no reason to quit but an indicator that you are heading in the right direction, because we must walk through the rain to see the rainbow and we must endure loss to make space for our new desired results.

Often the bigger the desired change , the bigger the pain, and this is why so few do it.

The very fact that are listening to this right now says to me you have something extra about you.

Inside you know there is more for you and that dream you have, you believe it is possible.

If others have done it before, then so can you , because we can do anything we set our minds and hearts to.

But we must take control of our destiny, have clear results in mind and take calculated action towards those results.

The path may be foggy and unknown but as you commit to the result and believe in it the path, it will be revealed soon enough.

We don't need to know the how, to declare we are going to do something, the how will come later.

Clear commitment to the result is key .

Too many people never live their dreams because they don't know how.

The how can be found out always if we can commit and believe fully in the process.

Faith is the magic elixir to success, without it nothing is possible.

What you believe about you is everything

If you believe you cannot swim and your dream is to be an Olympic swimming champion, what are your chances?

Any rational person would say, well learn to swim,

How many of you want to be multi-millionaires?

I guess everyone?

How many out there know how to get to such a status?

Would we just give up and say it is impossible?

Or would it be as logical as simply learning how to swim or ride a bike?

We believe someone could be an Olympic swimming champion with training and practice , but not a multi-millionaire?

Many of us think big goals are simply too unrealistic.

Fear of failure , fear of what people might think , fear of change , all common reasons for aiming low in life.

But when we aim low and succeed the disappointment in that success is a foul tasting medicine.

Start gaining clarity in the reality of our results.

By thinking bigger we all have the ability to hit what seem now like unrealistic heights, but later realise that nothing is impossible.

We should all start from the assumption that we can do anything, it might take years of training but we can do it. Anything we set our minds to, we can do it.

So ask yourself right now those very important questions.

What exactly would I be doing right now that will make me the happiest person in the world? How much money do I want?

What kind of relationships do I want?

When You have defined those things clearly,

Set the bar high and accept nothing less.

Because life will pay you any price.

But the time is ticking, you can't have it twice.

Chapter 10:
Trust The Process

Today we're going to talk about the power of having faith that things will work out for you even though you can't see the end in sight just yet. And why you need to simply trust in the process in all the things that you do.

Fear is something that we all have. We fear that if we quit our jobs to pursue our passions, that we may not be able to feed ourselves if our dreams do not work out. We fear that if we embark on a new business venture, that it might fail and we would have incurred financial and professional setbacks.

All this is borne out of the fear of the unknown. The truth is that we really do not know what can or will happen. We may try to imagine in our heads as much as we can, but we can never really know until we try and experienced it for ourselves.

The only way to overcome the fear of the unknown is to take small steps, one day at a time. We will, to the best of our ability, execute the plan that we have set for ourselves. And the rest we leave it up to the confidence that our actions will lead to results.

If problems arise, we deal with it there and then. We put out fires, we implement updated strategies, and we keep going. We keep going until we have exhausted all avenues. Until there is no more roads for us to travel, no more paths for us to create. That is the best thing that we can do.

If we constantly focus on the fear, we will never go anywhere. If we constantly worry about the future, we will never be happy with the present. If we dwell on our past failures, we will be a victim of our own shortcomings. We will not grow, we will not learn, we will not get better.

I challenge each and every one of you today to make the best out of every situation that you will face. Grab fear by the horns and toss them aside as if it were nothing. I believe in you and all that you can achieve.

Chapter 11:
Keep Moving When Things Get Hard

Keep to your goals by putting problems into perspective.

In times of difficulty, most give up.

Don't be like those people.

Difficulties are there to challenge us.

Difficulties are there to help us think outside the box.

Seek to change as you seek success.

Things never really stay the same.

Paths are never that straight.

You always come to a fork in the road.

Think of this new life and realise that thoughts will change how you act.

To have of a better life you must first consider losing this one you have now.

To achieve an extreme desired change you lose everything in the process.

It can be a tough pill to swallow.

It can be hard to see the silver lining.

But if you can keep moving towards what you have in mind,

sooner or later the new life will start to take shape.

First you must be unwavering in your faith.

It will get hard before it gets easy.
You must endure the winter to see the spring and summer.
You must weather the storm to see the sunshine.

Hard times come to all those who seek success.
Your courage will be tested.
Your endurance and persistence will be tested.
No one is exempt from this price.

You will find that nearly all your life's problems come from fear, loss, and pain,
but they are not as powerful as they appear.
They are no match for you if you believe that.
They are illusions.
Illusions because they are only real in our minds if we allow them to fester.

Most of your perceived problems never actually happened.
Most of your fears were phantoms of the mind.
Be prepared to lose it all if you desire a new life.

You must push through the pain to receive the gain.
In times of pain and struggle, you will grow.
In times of uncertainty, your bravery will shine through.
If you persist, you will make it through any problem.

You will become successful.

You must defeat the 3 phantoms to reach the promised land of health, happiness and wealth.

Self-mastery is not a battle with yourself.

Self-mastery is letting your inner-self take control.

The more you listen to your gut feeling the better your choices.

Your inner voice knows far more than your brain can tell you.

Problems arise because you have not taken action.

Force that change upon yourself.

You are like a shark.

You will die if you stop moving forward.

You will die if you accept defeat.

You must move forward like a shark.

No matter what,

Just keep swimming.

No matter what,

Get to your desired location

Get tough with yourself.

The outcome hangs in the balance.

Trust your inner compass to guide you.

Help who you can along the way.

Your thoughts will become reality good or bad.

Remain focus on the good despite the bad.

Lasting success is waiting for you.

YOU WILL MAKE IT as long as YOU DON'T QUIT!

Persistence is key.

Persist in getting what you want.

Persist in fighting for the job you desire.

Never give up even if you get rejected 100 times over.

Persistence always pays off.

You will be given your chance to shine if you keep at it.

Life will throw you curveballs.

As long as you are moving forward, you can still change direction.

Keep the dream in mind as you navigate through this uncharted territory.

No matter what,

Belief in yourself and your vision.

Keep trying to find the best people for your organisation and look after them like family.

One action can change your whole situation.

One action can change your entire life.

You will overcome the obstacles if you keep going and keep believing.

Nothing is more powerful than a made-up mind.

Chapter 12:
How To Use Military Strategy To Build Better Habits

What Is The Military?

Every country has a military. It is tasked with the duty of protecting the country's borders against external aggression and at times it quells internal violence or gets involved in rescue missions, both internally and externally. The men and women in uniform have a higher calling to serve and protect. Regardless of the nation they serve, they all have a common code of conduct they abide by.

Military Training

From recruitment to the hiring of personnel, military training is a serious affair. It is tough and no-nonsense. Their training is not limited to building their physical agility but also fortifying their mental strength and strategizing skills. They are trained through the most difficult situations and terrains and taught to withstand extremely harsh conditions.

Military strategies are full proof with almost zero chances of failure because they implement them to the latter or else they will have to pay with their lives on the battlefield. We can use such strategies to build better habits for ourselves and future generations.

Here are ways to use military strategies to build better habits:

1. <u>Discipline</u>

The military is also called the disciplined force because their discipline is unmatched. There is a clear hierarchy of protocol on who can issue what orders. There is no option of questioning orders from above; only their enforcement. Such streamlined command is lacking in the civilian world. Ironically, democracies are chaotic even when they are expected to be orderly because the majority have their say. This tendency makes progress slow and nothing can thrive. Good habits cannot blossom to bear fruits and the existing ones suffer a natural death.

At a personal level, uphold undemocratic military discipline if you want to succeed in building better habits. This kind of discipline acknowledges order and does not give room for action only when it is convenient. It is unpopular but functional.

Resolve to work on goals you had set without allowing excuses to slow you down. Be reasonable but ruthless in enforcing boundaries and work towards your goals. This is the type of military discipline that has been tried, tested, and proved to be working.

2. <u>Timekeeping</u>

Lack of punctuality has punctured the wheels of a majority of people. It is a chronic disease in our lives but the military has found its cure. Observe timeliness like your life depends on it. Punctuality will open doors you never knew existed in the first place. You build a reputation of a person possessing a rare quality – punctuality.

Broken promises, disappointments, unemployment, and missed business deals have partly been a product of lateness. We have disappointed the people we love and prospective business partners because we failed in keeping time.

The military knows better that timekeeping can save lives and seal the success of a mission. This is a strategy they have perfected. Instilling it in your life will create room to allow other positive habits to grow in your lives. Timeliness will make you stand out in this competitive world of slim chances.

3. <u>Physical Agility</u>

Physical agility is beyond appearance. It is a strategy that will ensure you fit in places where a majority of people do not. You will be flexible to run errands fast, and not get exhausted easily. It is difficult to find a physically unfit military officer. They are always in shape for them not to be a burden to their colleagues during training or on the battlefield.

It is a principal feature sought after in recruits. This strategy is a fertile ground for the development of better habits like exercising. The benefits of keeping fit to outweigh any inconveniences that you may encounter.

Other better habits like nutrition will be perfected if you work on physical agility. You will be physically fit if you have proper feeding habits. Military officers eat well-cooked balanced meals free of junk. This habit keeps them healthy and fit.

4. <u>Planning</u>

Planning is the master strategy because everything depends on it. A good plan is a job half done and the military knows better not to skip it. The enemy can have an undue advantage over soldiers with a weak plan or one full of loopholes. They will easily win in a war against a military starved of a solid plan. This makes it paramount to have a water-tight plan crafted beforehand and checked for anything not anticipated to be included.

Planning is a managerial function but the military has perfected it as a strategy mainly because their survival in war is dependent on how solid their plan is. You will not fall into bankruptcy if you plan well for your finances. Nobody wants to be a financial parasite on other people. Cure this with military-style planning.

Life is akin to a game of chess; one wrong move and you are at checkmate. You will build better spending, learning, and working habits if you plan your life properly. Look at the bigger picture before making key decisions lest you regret it when it is too late.

5. <u>Self-control</u>

How many times have you acted out of anger or happiness? Self-control is a trait that most civilians lack. We all have acted out of our emotions at one point. We vowed not to do one thing or another yet found ourselves back at it after a little while. This is caused by a lack of self-control.

Military training is where you are taught to detach yourself from your emotions. You instead reason with your mind, not your heart. This strategy has enabled officers to make reasonable decisions for the greater good of the team.

When a man can control his appetite for anything, he wields a lot of power. Many people lack self-control and they go ahead to satisfy their temporary gratifications. They end up losing all the gains they had made. It is possible to master self-control and act only when the time is right. The military does it and so can you. Take a cue from them.

In conclusion, better habits cannot be built from anywhere. They need to have a strong foundation. Military strategies are full proof and the best foundation you could get.

Chapter 13:
The Struggle With Time

Today we're going to talk about a topic that isn't commonly looked at in depth. But it is one that we might hopefully find a new appreciation for. And that is TIME.

Time is a funny thing, we are never really aware of it and how much of a limited resource it really is until we get a rude awakening. Most commonly when our mortality is tested. Whether it be a health scare, an accident, a death of a loved one, a death of a pet, we always think we have more time before that. That we will always have time to say i love you, to put off the things we always told ourselves we needed to do, to start making that change, to spend time with the people that mean the most to us.

As we go about our days, weeks and months, being bothered and distracted by petty work, by our bosses, colleagues, trying to climb the corporate ladder, we forget to stop and check in on our fiends and family… We forget that their time may be running out, and that we may not have as much time with them as we think we do, until it is too late, and then we regret not prioritising them first. All the money that we made could not ever buy back the time we have lost with them. And that is something we have to live with if we ever let that happen.

The other funny thing about time is that if we don't set it aside for specific tasks, if we don't schedule anything, we will end up wasting it on something mindless. Whether it be browsing social media endlessly, or bingeing on television, we will never run out of things to fill that time with. Can you imagine that even though time is so precious, we willingly sacrifice and trade it in for self isolation in front of our TVs and computers for hours on end. Sometimes even for days? Or even on mobile games. Some being so addictive that it consumes most of our waking hours if we are not careful.

Our devices have become dangerous time wasters. It is a tool Shea its literally sapping the living energy out of us. Which is why some responsible companies have started implementing new features that help us keep track of our screen time. To keep us in check, and to not let our children get sucked into this black hole that we might struggle to climb out of.

I believe the biggest struggle with time that we all have is how to spend it in such a way that we can be happy without feeling guilty. Guilty of not spending it wisely. And I believe the best way to start is to start defining the things that you need to do, and the things that you want to do. And then striking a balance. To set equal amounts of time into each activity so that it doesn't overwhelm or underwhelm you. Spend one hour on each activity each day that you feel will have an impact on your life in a meaningful way, and you can spend your time on television or games without remorse.

So I challenge each of you to make the most of your time. SPending time with loved ones always come first, followed by your goals and dreams, and then leisure activities. Never the other way around. That way you can be at the end of your life knowing that you had not wasted the most precious commodity that we are only given a finite amount of. Money can't buy back your youth, your health, or time with loved ones, so don't waste it.

Chapter 14:
How to Value Being Alone

Some people are naturally happy alone. But for others, being solo is a challenge. If you fall into the latter group, there are ways to become more comfortable with being alone (yes, even if you're a hardcore extrovert).

Regardless of how you feel about being alone, building a good relationship with yourself is a worthy investment. After all, you *do* spend quite a bit of time with yourself, so you might as well learn to enjoy it.

Being alone isn't the same as being lonely.

Before getting into the different ways to find happiness in being alone, it's important to untangle these two concepts: being alone and being lonely. While there's some overlap between them, they're completely different concepts. Maybe you're a person who basks in solitude. You're not antisocial, friendless, or loveless. You're just quite content with alone time. You look forward to it. That's simply being alone, not being lonely.

On the other hand, maybe you're surrounded by family and friends but not relating beyond a surface level, which has you feeling empty and disconnected. Or maybe being alone just leaves you sad and longing for company. That's loneliness.

Short-term tips to get you started

These tips are aimed at helping you get the ball rolling. They might not transform your life overnight, but they can help you get more comfortable with being alone.

Some of them may be exactly what you needed to hear. Others may not make sense to you. Use them as stepping-stones. Add to them and shape them along the way to suit your lifestyle and personality.

1. Avoid comparing yourself to others.

This is easier said than done, but try to avoid comparing your social life to anyone else's. It's not the number of friends you have or the frequency of your social outings that matters. It's what works for you.

Remember, you have no way of knowing if someone with many friends and a stuffed social calendar is happy.

2. Take a step back from social media.

Social media isn't inherently bad or problematic, but if scrolling through your feeds makes you feel left out and stresses, take a few steps back. That feed doesn't tell the whole story. Not by a long shot.

You have no idea if those people are truly happy or just giving the impression that they are. Either way, it's no reflection on you. So, take a [deep breath](#) and put it in perspective.

Perform a test run and ban yourself from social media for 48 hours. If that makes a difference, try giving yourself a daily limit of 10 to 15 minutes and stick to it.

Don't be afraid to ask for help.

Sometimes, all the self-care, exercise, and gratitude lists in the world aren't enough to shake feelings of sadness or loneliness.

Consider reaching out to a therapist if:

- You're overly stressed and finding it difficult to cope.
- You have symptoms of anxiety.
- You have symptoms of depression.

You don't have to wait for a crisis point to get into therapy. Simply wanting to get better and spending time alone is a perfectly good reason to make an appointment.

Chapter 15:
If You Commit to Nothing, You'll Be Distracted By Everything

I don't think anyone in their right mind would like to face a challenge where they have a chance to face failure or even a possibility of it.

We all need a new lesson to learn. A lesson of commitment and conviction. A lesson of integrity, grit, and sheer will. One might ask, why should I adopt the features of a soldier rather than a normal social being. Why do I need to go to extremes?

The answer to these questions is simple yet heavy, with a load most people avoid their whole life.

We all have somewhat similar goals. We all want to be in a better place in better shape. We all want wealth. We all want healthy stable relationships. We all want respect and a million other things.

Ask yourself this; Have you ever actually tried hard enough for any of this to happen. Have you ever tried to dig deep till you found your last breath? But it felt good because you had a good enough reason and passion to pursue?

The goals of life are a compulsion to have. We all must have something to strive for. Something worth fighting for. Something we can look back and be happy about.

But having a goal and committing to it are two different things.

One can have a goal and still not be motivated enough to do anything in their power to achieve that thing. No matter how the road takes turns.

We need to have the inspiration to drive us through the rough patches of life. To make us keep pushing even if we get squeezed within the incidents happening around us.

Don't take this the wrong way but you have to accept the fact that whatever you are feeling has nothing to do with what you want to achieve. Because what you want to achieve is something that your life depends on. The goals you set aren't some wishes or a feeling that your gut gives you. These goals are the requirements of life with which you can finally say lived a happy successful life. And this statement is the ultimate purpose of your life.

You were given this life because you had the energy to go for things that weren't easy, but you had the potential to achieve these. All you needed was a little commitment and Zero distractions.

The commitment you need isn't a feeling that goes and on and off like a switch. Rather a distinct key for the lock of your life.

So if you still think you will have days where you can try one more time, Let me be clear; You better start thinking about the future of your next generation. Because I don't think they'd have one.

You need to be committed enough to do anything that takes you closer and closer to your goals and nothing that wastes a second out of your life.

Because either you go all in or you walk the line and hedge your bets. The bet here being your life.

Chapter 16:
How To Stick To Your Goals When Life Gets Crazy

<u>Life Can Be Rocky</u>

We all can agree that life can sometimes be noisy and messy. It can be chaos and madness and a single voice of reason in a room may lack. When life gets crazy, priorities change, and goalposts are sometimes shifted in the heat of the moment. Life is indiscriminate of your age or gender and it can turn your goals upside down.

Sanity vanishes in thin air when life is marred by confusion. In this state, you will most likely replace your goals with others because they look more relevant and probably easily attainable.

Many people abandon 'fragile' goals when life gets bumpy. Some argue that a mouth-to-hand lifestyle is not ideal when chasing after your goals. Do not get mixed up in this confusion, retreat to sobriety and ask yourself whether you will do the blame game or work towards your goals. Be assertive with yoursrightelf.

<u>Get Your Priorities</u>

Define your goals and how you intend to follow up on each one to completion. You cannot stick to vague goals. They have to be clear in your mind and the route to chase after them should be outlined awaiting execution. The common mistake most people commit is to say they will cross the bridge when they get there. This form of procrastination is misleading. Live the present and plan for the future.

A good plan is a job half done. Nothing should steal your focus from knowing your priorities. Not even the craze of life. Prioritize what is important and snob anything outside the plan no matter how lucrative or tempting it may present itself.

Have Well-Founded Goals

The foundation of your goals matters the most in determining whether you will stick to them or not. Some people set unrealistic goals because of external influence and peer pressure. If you fall within this category, you will be chasing after an illusion and living a lie because your dreams are not in tandem with your personality.

Well-founded goals go beyond convenience. You set them based on your ability and vision of how you want to live your life. It should be devoid of exaggeration and imitation of the lifestyles of celebrities. You will be able to stick to your goals if you are true to yourself.

Authenticity and fidelity to the kind of person you are will glue you to your goals. Is not that the dream you want to live?

Superfluous goals are changed from time to time for convenience. Question your commitment to your goals when you start shifting goalposts.

Have A Thorough Understanding Of Your Environment

We are products of our environments. The role your environment plays in your life cannot be ignored. A toxic and unfriendly environment is incapable of manifesting your good goals. Instead, it will poison you to turn your back on the goals you had set. You may be a good person with pure intentions but your environment waters down all the gains you could achieve.

It is beneficial to exist in a good environment. It will channel positive energy your way to incubate your goals to their manifestation. Take time to understand your work or home environment and alienate yourself from any negative influence. It is better to be safe than sorry.

If circumstances demand, you can change your residence just to have a clear head to enable you to stick to your goals. Embrace positivity and watch yourself grow into the person you intend to be.

Audit Your List of Friends

Have you ever heard of the saying that you are the average of your five friends? The impact of your friends on your life cannot be underscored. They, in cahoots with your environment, have the potential to ensure whether or not you stick to and realize your goals.

Sit down to rethink the type of people you consider to be your friends. If they are wayward, they will pull you away from your goals. They will want you to be like them and possibly make you abandon your goals if they do not align with theirs.

Your success in sticking to your goals even when life gets crazy is pegged on your choice of associates. Choose them carefully.

Consume Inspirational and Motivational Content

Sometimes we need some positive energy in our lives to lift our spirits and soothe us that everything will be alright. Following your goals is a bumpy ride if there is nobody to encourage you. Read, listen and watch success stories to be encouraged.

Sticking to your goals is a conscious decision one makes and works towards it daily. You need a voice of reason to rise above that of discouragement. Finally, reason prevails and you get encouraged even when at the brink of giving up.

In conclusion, it has become the norm for life to get crazy. Responsibilities bombard us right, left, and center. You need to be inseparable from your goals for you to achieve them.

Chapter 17:
How To Find Your Passion

Today we're going to talk about a topic that i think many of you are interested to know about. And that is how to find your passion.

For many of us, the realities of work and obligations means that we end up doing something we dislike for the money in the hopes that it might buy us some happiness. That sometimes we stop following our passion because maybe it does not exactly pay very well. And that is a fair decision to make.

But today, i hope to be able to help you follow at least one passion project at any point in your life in the hopes that it might help elevate your spirits, give your life more meaning, and help you live each day with a renewed drive and purpose.

You see, the world can be very dull if we chase something that we actually don't really feel attracted to. For example, when we are forced to do something out of sheer dread day in and day out, it will suck the living soul out of us and we will tend to fall into the trap of running an endless wheel with no hope in sight. When we chase material things for example, money or luxury products, we sell our soul to a job that pays well physically but not emotionally and spiritually. As a human being, we have traded our very essence and time, for a piece of paper or digital currency that serves no purpose than to enrich us externally. While it might feel good to be living comfortably, past a certain threshold, there is a point of diminishing returns. And more money just doesn't bring you that much joy anymore.

Yes you may have the fanciest, car, house, and whatever physical possessions you have. But how many of you have heard stories of people who have a lot of money but end up depressed, or end up blowing it all away because they can never spend enough to satisfy their cravings for physical goods and services. What these people lacked in emotional growth, they tried to overcompensate with money. And as their inner self gets emptier and emptier, they themselves get poorer and poorer as well.

On the flip side, many would argue that passion is overrated. That passion is nothing but some imaginary thing that we tell ourselves we need to have in order to be happy. But i am here to argue that you do not need to make passion your career in order to be happy.

You see, passion is an aspiration, passion is something that excites you, passion is something that you would do even if it does not pay a single cent. That you would gladly trade your time readily for even if it meant u weren't getting anything monetary in return. Because this passion unlocks something within you that cannot be explained with being awarded physical prizes. It is the feeling that you are truly alive and happy, you are so incredibly grateful and thankful to be doing at that very moment in time, that nothing else mattered, not even sleep.

To me, and I hope you will see this too, that passion can be anything you make it out to be. It can be something as simple as a passion for singing, a passion for creating music, a passion for helping others, passion for supporting your family, passion for starting a family, passion for doing charity work, passion for supporting a cause monetarily, or even a passion for living life to the fullest and being grateful each day.

For some lucky ones, they have managed to marry their passion with their career. They have somehow made their favourite thing to do their job, and it fulfills them each day. To those people, i congratulate you and envy you.

But for the rest of us, our passion can be something we align our soul with as long as it fulfils us as well. If we have multiple mouths to feed, we can make our passion as being the breadwinner to provide for our family if it brings us joy to see them happy. If we have a day job that we hate but can't let go off for whatever reasons, we can have a passion for helping others, to use the income that we make to better the lives of others.

And for those who have free time but are not sure what to do with it, to just simply start exploring different interests and see what hobbies you resonate with. You may never know what you might discover if you did a little digging.

What I have come to realize is that passions rarely stay the same. They change as we change, they evolve over time just as we grow. And many of the passions we had when we were younger, we might outgrow them when we hit a certain age. As our priorities in life change, our passions follow along.

In my opinion, you do not need to make your passion your career in order to be truly happy.. I believe that all you need is to have at least 1 passion project at any given point of time in your life to sustain you emotionally and spiritually. Something that you can look forward to on your off days, in your time away from work, that you can pour all your time and energy into willingly without feeling that you have wasted any second. And who knows, you might feel so strongly about that passion project that you might even decide to make it your career some day. The thing is you never really know. Life is mysterious like that.

All I do know is that chasing money for the wrong reasons will never net u happiness. But having a passion, whatever it may be, will keep you grounded and alive.

So I challenge each and everyone of you today to look into your current life, and see there are any bright spots that you have neglected that you could revive and make it your passion project. Remember that passion can be anything you make out to be as long as you derive fulfilment and happiness from it. Helpfully one that isnt material or monetary.

Chapter 18:
How To Simplify Your Life And Maximise Your Results

The word "simplicity" seems almost like a single-word oxymoron. The fast-paced, tech-driven world we live in makes it almost impossible to keep it simple. More and more apps are created every day to help make daily tasks such as communicating, shopping, and budgeting simpler – but the truth is, life these days couldn't be more complex.

We can agree that on most days, 24 hours just isn't enough time to get it all done, even though our multi-tasking skills are at their max. There is a widespread *need* for a simpler routine, but achieving success where that's concerned, is complicated. Where do you even start? (See, even the first step is hard!)

The Pareto principle, commonly known as the 80/20 rule, is a rule that has been universally accepted to explain the balance of output vs. input. The 80/20 rule states that 80% of results come from 20% of the action in a simple sentence. The 80/20 rule has proven to be true time and time again in many aspects of business such as economics, sales, real estate, health and safety, information technology, and sports.

How does this apply to you? It boils down to 80% of overall output -or- your accomplishments, at home, at work, in the gym, etc., comes from 20% of input -or- focused time, energy, and effort. So, in other words, to make the simplest and most effective strides to your goals, you have to focus on the *right* 20%. Clear as mud? Okay, let's look at an example. Have you ever known someone who tends to keep busy all the time but never really gets anything accomplished? That is because they are taking the path of least resistance, working on lots of little things that don't have a high value or return. Prioritizing quick, trivial, or less effective tasks over more difficult, time-consuming, yet impactful tasks is the procrastination paradox that leads to running in circles but never getting things done.

What's the solution? Goal prioritization and time management. Try this exercise to help simplify your goal and task list down to what matters to you.

1. Make a list of 10 things you want to accomplish in the next 30 days – in no particular order. These ten goals can apply to any area of your life – personal or professional. (The first of a new month is a great time to try this for the first time.)

2. Assign a category to each goal – family/friends, career, personal, etc.

3. Review the list carefully, considering the areas of your life each goal will impact. Now rank these 10 goals from 1-10; 1 = most important, 10 = least important.

If you are going to take Bruce Lee's path to simplicity by "hacking away at the unessential," – first determine what *is essential* (AKA rank your goals and priorities) and then start to remove the small barriers in your path that you can control.

Chapter 19:
Motivate Yourself

Motivation is a multibillion dollar industry.

There are many great motivational materials to help keep you motivated.

Some of the motivational material is great and should be studied and applied but this kind of motivation is what I call push, which is a good start, but in combination with pull motivation,(your personal why and reason), you can reach your goals faster.

With the use of videos, books , audio material and concentrating on your reasons, the sky really is the limit.

Using what works for you, which may be different than what works for others.

Motivation is very much personal to you.

Work with what pulls you and pushes you to reach your goals on record time.

Pushing and pulling everyday until your dream becomes reality.

The pull is your WHY , the big reason for taking action in the first place.

The pull is the motivations that effect you personally, and the big fire that will help your dream burn , even through the storms and the rain.

Using the push motivators in conjunction to maximize your motivation on all fronts.

Create as much of your dream around you as you can with what you have right now to make it seem more real.

Pictures , music , videos, foods, smells , clothing.

Whatever you can do to create it now.

The engine to drive you there may not have arrived yet, but don't close the factory, work on the interior and bodywork, because your engine is on the way.

You know what you want, you know the first steps, take them in confidence, not fear.

If the dream is here, it is already real if you just believe and move towards it.

With motivation , self determination and faith you have already won the race before it has even begun.

Setting up the ideal environment for the garden of your life to flourish.

Strengthen the desire, strengthen the belief.

Motivation in the mind without belief in the heart will only lead to disappointment.

Your why must be something close to the heart for you to endure the tribulations of champions.

Your motivations must be clear and personal.

Defining your purpose, often money alone will not make us happy.

The money must have a greater personal purpose to bring you happiness.

Giving often feels more rewarding than recieving.

As living a truthful life is more rewarding than decieving.

The key to your dreams is often what you are believing.

Believing in yourself and your capabilities is key.

You can study every bit of motivational material ever made, but if you don't believe in yourself, you can not be successful.

Self belief and self motivation are far stronger than the push of what we can learn from the outside.

Let the outside information light the fire as it is intended, be a keen learner of what is relevant, and motivate yourself by concentrating on what is important to you.

Motivate yourself , health, happiness and wealth.

Its possible for you now.

If you believe and push to achieve.

Chapter 20:
How To Focus and Concentrate On Your Work

Today we're going to talk about a topic that I think everyone struggles with, including myself. Being able to sit in front of your computer for hours on end is not something that comes naturally to anyone, well not for me anyway.

Unfortunately, this is a skill that needs to be learned. And it is on some level crucial for our career success. So if this is something that you struggle with, then stick around for the rest of the video to learn how you can increase your level of concentration and to be more productive.

So what is focus and how do we get more of it?

The first thing we need to know is that focus is a state of mind. Without getting into too scientific terms, focus happens when our brains generate certain waves, I'm sure you've heard of alpha, theta, beta, waves. But to get to this state, we must give it some time. And the first step is to simply start sitting on your desk and practicing some deep breathing to get you prepared for that state. Close your eyes, just take some time to focus on your breath and nothing else. Feel your body calming down from a more excitable state, to one of more serenity and peace. Let go of any thoughts that come your way, whatever problems that crosses your mind, just let it flow away. If you need to take some time to do so right now, just pause the video and practice this deep breathing for yourself. For those that require a more holistic practice, you can check out my meditation link here, where you will be guided through a simple 10 min practice to get yourself in the right state of mind.

The next thing we need to know about focus is that it requires us to be free from distraction. When we get interrupted in our workflow by distractions such as buzzing from our phones, social media, by other people, or even our pets, we break the momentum that we have so painstakingly built. According to Newton's Law: The law states that as object at rest will stay at rest, an object in motion will stay in motion unless acted on by a net external force. The same principle applies to our focus, when we break that motion, it will take an equal amount of energy to get us back on track again. So to save our brains from having to work extra hard to keep you concentrated, it is vital that we eliminate all possible sources of distraction that will pull us away from the state of focus. It is best that we set aside at least 1-2 hours of our time where nothing and no one can disturb us. Do not schedule your meals or coffee break in between those times of concentration as the same principle applies to those as well.

The final thing we need to know is that focus is a muscle, and the more that we train it each day, the easier it gets for us to get into that state. I believe that focus, as with anything else, requires a daily routine for us to get into the habit of being able to switch quickly from play to work. As you train yourself to be more focused, by first being more attentive to the various nuances of how to achieve focus, it will come more naturally to us if we keep applying the same practice for 10, 20, 30 days in a row. When we make a conscious effort to keep distractions away, when we find less excuses to wander around our work place, when we make it a point that we will do our very best to stay focused each and every day, it will come as no surprise that your levels of productivity and concentration will definitely increase. Our brain's capacity for staying in that state of mind will increase as well. And hopefully we will be more creative and innovative as a result.

I want to give you one more bonus tip to help you get the ball rolling, if you find you need an extra boost. That is to think of the rewards that being focused can get you. Try your best to visualise the benefits of being productive and getting your work out of the way, the time you will have after to do the things you enjoy, if work isnt one of them. The friends that you can see after the work is done, and how much time you won't have to waste being distracted and spending your whole day in front of your computer only to realise you only put in 2 hours of actual work in. Also think of the monetary rewards maybe of being focused, how much more money you can potentially be earning, or how many clients and business deals can you close if you just became more productive. You can even think of the intrinsic rewards of being focused, how proud would you be of yourself if you had actually done the 5-6 hours of work that you promised you would do.

So for those who are struggling with focus and concentration, I challenge you to take a look at the surroundings of your workplace... What can you do to minimise the distractions, and how can you get and stay in that focused state of mind for longer without letting your concentration drift away.

I believe that you can do anything that you set your mind to. So go out there and achieve focus like never before.

Chapter 21:

Happy People Take Care of Themselves

I frequently hear the word "selfish" tossed about in coaching, often with a negative connotation. Someone feels bad that they were selfish or that someone else was selfish, and it was offensive. Selfishness – the lack of considering others or only being concerned with your advantage – can be a great weakness. The ability to put others' needs in front of your own is an important life skill that you need to be able to do without resentment, even when it's completely inconvenient and a sacrifice.

However, I would argue that the motivation behind that decision should be self-serving. In most cases, being selfish is just a matter of perspective, critical to happiness and self-evolution.

Let me explain…

First, let's talk about why it is so important to be selfish. As author <u>Brené Brown</u> has discovered in her research on wholehearted living, loving yourself more than you love others is the first and most critical step to seeking happiness and fulfillment.

She says it is impossible to love anyone more than you love yourself. Taking care of yourself is the pathway to fulfillment and high performance in work and life. And, just as importantly, it's a gift to others.

When your needs are met, and you feel good about yourself, it's easier to elevate other people's needs in front of your own. It's easy to be a giver when your cup is full. When you feel half-full or empty, it's harder to give. You inherently feel people should be giving more to you or others, so you don't have to give so much or feel you need to preserve more for yourself.

Here are the two common derailments that can prevent you from finding fulfillment:

1. Giving too much

When people give too much - continually put other people's needs ahead of their own - builds resentment and takes away from their ability to take care of themselves. When their time is so focused on others, they don't have any time left for themselves. I find people do this when they are uncomfortable asking for their needs, speaking up about issues, or delegating responsibilities. Often they hide these weaknesses by focusing on other people, so they don't have to focus on themselves. This not only leads to feeling unfulfilled but becomes a burden on others who feel they need to take care of the "giver."

2. Taking too much time for ourselves

On the opposite end of the spectrum, some people take too much time for themselves, mistakenly thinking it will lead to fulfillment. They do not "give" enough, and it usually makes them feel worse, disengaging them from relationships and putting them on a treadmill of trying to do something that will finally make them feel good. In these cases, they are usually working on the wrong issues. The places where they are investing their time do not give them meaning.

Chapter 22:
Happy People Surround Themselves with The Right People

Whether we realized it or not, we become like the five people we spend the most time with. We start behaving like them, thinking like them, looking like them. We even make decisions based on what we think they would want us to do.

For example, there are many research findings that prove we are more likely to gain weight if a close friend or a family member becomes overweight. Similarly, we are more likely to engage in an exercise program if we surround ourselves with fit and health-oriented people.

So, who are the top 5 influencers in your life? Do they make you feel positive? Do they inspire and motivate you to be the best version of yourself? Do they support and encourage you to achieve your goals? Or, do they tell you that "it can't be done," "it's not possible," "you aren't good enough," "you will most likely fail."

If you feel emotionally drained by the energetic vampires in your life, you may want to detox your life and get rid of the relationships that aren't serving you in a positive way.

The negative people, the naysayers, the Debbie Downers, and the chronic complainers are like a dark cloud over your limitless potential.

They hold you back and discourage you from even trying because they're afraid that if you succeed, you'll prove them wrong.

Have the courage to remove the negative people from your life and watch how your energy and enthusiasm automatically blossom. Letting go of the relationships that aren't serving us is a critical step if we want to become more positive, fulfilled, and successful.

Detoxing your life from negative influencers will also allow you to become the person you truly want to be. You'll free yourself from constant judgment, negativity, and lack of support.

Here's what you can do:

- Stay away from chronic complainers.
- Stop participating in meaningless conversations.
- Share your ideas only with people who are supportive or willing to provide constructive criticism.
- Minimize your interactions with "friends," coworkers, and family members who are negative, discouraging, and bitter.
- Stop watching TV and reading negative posts on social media (yes, mainstream media is a major negative influence in our lives!).
- Surround yourself with positive and successful people (remember, we become like the top 5 people we spend our time with!).

- Find new, like-minded friends, join networking and support groups, or find a positive coach or a mentor.

If you want to make a positive change in your life, remember, the people around you have a critical influence on your energy, growth, and probability of success.

Positive people bring out the best in you and make you feel motivated and happy. They help you when you're in need, encourage you to go after your dreams, and are there to celebrate your successes or support you as you move past your challenges. Pick your top 5 wisely!

Chapter 23:
It's Not Your Job to Tell Yourself "No"

How many times have you had the chance to go around something that could have changed your life? What were your thoughts when you decided to enter a state where even the slightest thought of failure leads you to stop acting on it?

I'm sure every one of us has a good reason behind everything we opt to do or don't in our lives.

But there is never a good enough reason to back down just because we have some examples of failures on our hands.

No one can decide what reality and nature have decided for them. Everyone must learn to juggle life and play with every piece they get a hand on.

Everything in life is meant to be taken as a risk. You can never learn to swim till you get your first dive in a deep pool. You never learn to ride a bike till you have no one behind you to stop you from falling.

Everyone needs a bump every now and then. And when you finally decide to hike that hurdle, you finally start to see the horizon.

We all seem to get depressed more easily than we start to get motivated. We seem to get carried away with every stone that life throws back at us but we never try to catch that stone. We never try to indulge in one more suffering just to get better at what we are tested with.

Nobody wants to fail and that's why no one wants to take a chance at what might fail.

The mere fear of facing failure makes us build a mechanism of self-defense that forces us to say 'No' to anything that might hurt us one day.

But the reality is that it is illogical to stop just so you are afraid to face the reality. The reality is that you are a sane human and this is life. Life tests us in ways hardly imaginable.

When you say 'No' to yourself, it rarely means 'Not Now'. It always means 'Maybe some other time'. But deep down we already know that we will never attempt to do that thing. At least not consciously.

We always try for the best. We try to be the best at what we already have and are already doing. We are motivated enough to try new things, things that are more scary and unknown to us.

What we really should be doing is to try and get a taste of newer victories. Trying to search for new horizons. Trying to get what most fail to achieve. Because every other man or woman is just like us, afraid to fail and avoiding embarrassment. Our embarrassments are mostly self-imposed and we are the better judge of our failures.

There is no motivation and inspiration more powerful in the world than the spark that ignites within you.

Our sole purpose in life is to embrace everything that we come across. It is never to prevent something just because you don't have the courage to face your failures yet.

Chapter 24: Happy People Use Their Character Strengths

One of the most popular exercises in the science of positive psychology (some argue it is the single most popular exercise) is referred to as "use your signature strengths in new ways." But what does this exercise mean? How do you make the most of it to benefit yourself and others?

On the surface, the exercise is self-explanatory:

a. Select one of your highest strengths – one of your **character strengths** that is core to who you are, is easy for you to use, and gives you energy;
b. Consider a new way to express the strength each day;
c. Express the strength in a new way each day for at least 1 week.

Studies repeatedly show that this exercise is connected with long-term benefits (e.g., 6 months) such as higher levels of happiness and lower levels of depression.

PUT THE EXERCISE INTO PRACTICE

In practice, however, people sometimes find it surprisingly challenging to come up with new ways to use one of their signature strengths. This is because we are very accustomed to using our strengths. We frequently use our strengths mindlessly without much awareness. For example, have you paid much attention to your use of self-regulation as you brush your teeth? Your level of prudence or kindness while driving? Your humility while at a team meeting?

For some strengths, it is easy to come up with examples. Want to apply **curiosity** in a new way? Below is a sample mapping of what you might do. Keep it simple. Make it complex. It's up to you!

- On Monday, take a new route home from work and explore your environment as you drive.
- On Tuesday, ask one of your co-workers a question you have not previously asked them.
- On Wednesday, try a new food for lunch – something that piques your curiosity to taste.
- On Thursday, call a family member and explore their feelings about a recent positive experience they had.
- On Friday, take the stairs instead of the elevator and explore the environment as you do.
- On Saturday, as you do one household chore (e.g., washing the dishes, vacuuming), pay attention to 3 novel features of the activity while you do it. Example: Notice the whirring sound of the vacuum, the accumulation of dust swirling around in the container, the warmth of the water as you wash the dishes, the sensation of the weight of a single plate or cup, and so on.

- On Sunday, ask yourself 2 questions you want to explore about yourself – reflect or journal your immediate responses.
- Next Monday....keep going!

WIDENING THE SCOPE

In some instances, you might feel challenged to come up with examples. Let me help. After you choose one of your signature strengths, consider the following 10 areas to help jolt new ideas within you and stretch your approach to the strength.

How might I express the character strength...

- At work
- In my closest relationship
- While I engage in a hobby
- When with my friends
- When with my parents or children
- When I am alone at home
- When I am on a team
- As the leader of a project or group
- While I am driving
- While I am eating

Chapter 25:
How to Stop Chasing New Goals All the Time

The philosopher Alan Watts always said that life is like a song, and the sole purpose of the song is to dance. He said that when we listen to a song, we don't dance to get to the end of the music. We dance to enjoy it. This isn't always how we live our lives. Instead, we rush through our moments, thinking there's always something better, there's always some goal we need to achieve.

"Existence is meant to be fun. It doesn't go anywhere; it just is."
Our lives are not about things and status. Even though we've made ourselves miserable with wanting, we already have everything we need. Life is meant to be lived. If you can't quit your job tomorrow, enjoy where you are. Focus on the best parts of every day. Believe that everything you do has a purpose and a place in the world.

Happiness comes from <u>gratitude</u>. You're alive, you have people to miss when you go to work, and you get to see them smile every day. We all have to do things we don't want to do; we have to survive. When you find yourself working for things that don't matter, like a big house or a fancy car, when you could be living, you've missed the point. You're playing the song, but you're not dancing.

"A song isn't just the ending. It's not just the goal of finishing the song. The song is an experience."

We all think that everything should be amazing when we're at the top, but it's not. Your children have grown older, and you don't remember the little things.

"...tomorrow and plans for tomorrow can have no significance at all unless you are in full contact with the reality of the present since it is in the present and only in the present that you live."

You feel cheated of your time, cheated by time. Now you have to make up for it. You have to live, make the most of what you have left. So you set another goal.

This time you'll build memories and see places, do things you never got the chance to do. The list grows, and you wonder how you'll get it all done and still make your large mortgage payment. You work more hours so you can do all this stuff "someday." You've overwhelmed yourself again.

You're missing the point.

Stop wanting more, <u>be grateful for</u> today. Live in the moment. Cherish your life and the time you have in this world. If it happens, it happens. If it doesn't, then it wasn't meant to; let it go.

"We think if we don't interfere, it won't happen."

There's always an expectation, always something that has to get done. You pushed aside living so that you could live up to an expectation that doesn't exist to anyone but you. The expectation is always there because you gave it power. To live, you've got to let it go.

You save all your money so that you can retire. You live to retire. Then you get old, and you're too tired to live up to the expectation you had of retirement; you never realize your dreams.

At forty, you felt cheated; at eighty, you are cheated. You cheated yourself the whole way through to the end.

"Your purpose was to dance until the end, but you were so focused on the end that you forgot to dance."

Chapter 26: Happy People View Problems as Challenges

To state the obvious: It's easier to be happy when things are going well. Positive outcomes are known to lift people's moods, while negative emotions (like anxiety) generally reflect concerns about negative outcomes.

But, happy people are also good at dealing with problems in ways that help them to maintain their mood, while still dealing with issues effectively. Here are three common things that happy people tend to do to deal with speed bumps in life.

FOCUS ON THE FUTURE

It is important to understand the problem you're facing, and so happy people certainly analyze the situation. But, they don't remain focused on the problem for long. That is, they avoid rumination—which is a set of repeated thoughts about something that has gone wrong.

Instead, they look to the future. There are two benefits to this: One is that the future is not determined yet, and so happy people can be optimistic about things to come. The other is that happy people are looking to make the future better than the past, which creates a hopeful outlook—no matter what the present circumstances look like.

FIND AGENCY

At any given moment, the situation you are in exerts some amount of control over your options. When you're sitting in traffic, for example, there isn't much you can do but wait for the cars around you to start moving. The amount of control you have to take action in a situation is your degree of agency.

Happy people seek out their sources of agency when problems arise. They are most interested in what they can do to influence the situation, rather than focusing on all of the options that have been closed off by what has happened. The focus on agency is important, because it provides the basis for creating a plan to solve the problem. And the sooner a problem is addressed, the less time it has to cause stress.

KNOW WHEN TO FOLD

There are always going to be big problems that you can't solve. Perhaps there is a client who is never satisfied with the work you do. Maybe there is a process you're trying to implement that never seems to have the desired outcome. You might even have been working on the problem for a long time.

Despite all the discussions about the importance of grit, effective (and happy) problem solvers are good at knowing when to walk away from a problem that can't be fixed. Each of us has a limited amount of time and energy that we can devote to the work we are doing. Spending time on problems that cannot be solved has an opportunity cost. There are other things you could be doing with your time that might yield better outcomes. It is important to learn when it is time to give up on a problem rather than continuing to try to solve it.

This is particularly true when you have been working on that problem for a long time. There is a tendency for people to pay attention to sunk costs—the time, money, and energy they have already devoted to working on something. But, those resources are gone, and you can't get them back. If it isn't likely that additional effort is going to help you solve a problem, then you should walk away, no matter how hard you have worked on it already. Happy people are good at ignoring those sunk costs both when making the decision to walk away from a project and after making the decision to walk away. They don't spend time regretting the "wasted" resources.

Chapter 27:

It's Okay To Feel Uncertain

We are surrounded by a world that has endless possibilities. A world where no two incidents can predict the other. A realm where we are a slave to the unpredictable future and its repercussions.

Everyone has things weighing on their mind. Some of us know it and some of us keep carrying these weights unknowingly.

The uncertainty of life is the best gift that you never wanted. But when you come to realize the opportunities that lie at every uneven corner are worth living for.

Life changes fast, sometimes in our favor and sometimes not much. But life always has a way to balance things out. We only need to find the right approach to make things easier for us and the ones around us.

Everyone gets tested once in a while, but we need to find ways to cope with life when things get messy.

The worst thing the uncertainty of life can produce is the fear in your heart. The fear to never know what to expect next. But you can never let fear rule you.

To worry about the future ahead of us is pointless. So change the question from 'What if?' to 'What will I do if.'

If you already have this question popping up in your brain, this means that you are already getting the steam off.

You don't need to fear the uncertain because you can never wreck your life in any such direction from where there is no way back.

The uncertainty of life is always a transformation period to make you realize your true path. These uncertainties make you realize the faults you might have in your approach to things.

You don't need to worry about anything unpredictable and unexpected because not everything is out of your control every time. Things might not happen in a way you anticipated but that doesn't mean you cannot be prepared for it.

There are a lot of things that are in your control and you are well researched and well equipped to go around events. So use your experience to do the damage control.

Let's say you have a pandemic at your hand which you couldn't possibly predict, but that doesn't mean you cannot do anything to work on its effects. You can raise funds for the affected population. You can try to find new ways to minimize unemployment. You can find alternate ways to keep the economy running and so on.

Deal with your emotions as you cannot get carried away with such events being driven by your feelings.

Don't avoid your responsibilities and don't delay anything. You have to fulfill every task expected of you because you were destined to do it. The results are not predetermined on a slate but you can always hope for the best be the best version of yourself no matter how bad things get.

Life provides us with endless possibilities because when nothing is certain, anything is possible. So be your own limit.

Chapter 28: Consistency

Today we're going to talk about a very important topic that I believe is one of the core principles that we should all strive to integrate into our lives. And that is consistency.

What does consistency mean to you when you hear that word? For me previously when I kept hearing people say that I would need to stay consistent in this and that, it did not ring any bells in me and i brushed it off thinking it was just another productivity word similar to work hard, be positive and so on. However it was only when I start doing more digging that I realized that many successful people in life actually attributed consistency as being the key factor that led to their success. That it was that one quality they possessed in their work ethic that allowed them to surpass their competition. That they had set out a plan and stuck to it consistency over days, months, years, and even decades until they finally achieved their goals.

You see for many of us, consistency is something that i believe we all struggle with. Whether it be going to the gym, putting in the effort to work out, going for trainings, health wise or work related, studying, practicing an instrument, especially things we find to be not so enjoyable to do, we just do not show up consistently enough to produce results that are satisfactory let alone ones that we are proud of.

And we complain that our body doesn't look good, that we are getting nowhere with learning a new instrument, or maybe that we have plateaued in the area that we most wish to desire to move forward in, work or play.

You see, your level of consistency is directly correlated with the amount of time you actually spend on an activity. And if your consistency drops, it is no wonder that your performance drops as well as you are not putting in the adequate amount of time to actually progress forward. As the saying goes, practice makes perfect. And Practice takes time. And time requires consistency.

Highly successful figures in any field, be it sports or the business world, from roger Federer, Lionel Messi, Michael jordan, Kobe Bryant, to Elon Musk, Bill Gates, Steve Jobs, they possess a strong vision for themselves and their consistency is a tool for their success. They would not hesitate to put every ounce of their time and energy into being the best in their field by showing up every single day for practice or for work, to get better each day and to crush their opinion. What they lack in skill, they make up for in consistency in practice. And they improve much faster than their opponents as a result, keeping them at the very top level of their game.

With the knowledge that consistency was the key to success for many entrepreneurs and businessmen, i decided to try it out for myself. Previously I was erratic in my work schedule. I always wandered around my tasks and never put in the effort to put in a set number of hours every day. I felt that my body wasn't getting any fitter, my tennis was average at best, and my income never really went anywhere. In all areas of my life, it felt like i had reached a ceiling.

After making the change to becoming more consistent in everything that I did, I saw a marked improvement in all areas that I had struggled with previously. My body started taking shape, my tennis game improved, and my income grew as well. The thing is, i hadn't done anything different apart from making it a daily habit and routine of putting in more hours into each task, showing up for more gym sessions, showing up for more tennis games, showing up for more hours at work, and consistently putting out more content. While gradual, these hours slowly added up and I saw a breakthrough. And I was surprised at how one small little change in how I approached life actually benefited me. I felt happier that i was improving in all these areas, and it had a snowball effect of actually compounding over time. Sooner or later i was beating my peers in all areas that I was once level with.

I challenge each and everyone of you to make consistency one of your core philosophies in life. To approach each and every task, project, or mission you embark on with a level of consistency unmatched by those around you. I am sure you will be very surprised at what you can achieve with just this one simple tweak in everything that you do.

Chapter 29:
Happy People Stay Grateful For Everything They Have

A lot of us will have different answers to this simple question, "what are you grateful for today?" It could differ from as simple as getting out of bed to achieving that huge task you had your mind on for a while. Gratitude is the emotion we feel when we tend to notice and appreciate the good things that have come into our lives. Some people feel grateful for even the tiniest things, while others don't even if they achieve more than they have wished for. Most of the time, people who will be thankful still feel negative emotions, but they tend to shift their focus from all the bad things in their lives to the good ones.

Research has shown that teenagers and adults who feel more grateful than others are also happier, get better grades, have better friends, get more opportunities, have fewer illnesses and pain, have more energy, and tend to sleep better. The link of practicing gratitude to achieve happiness is through a path that we commonly call the "cognitive pathway." The words "cognitive" and "cognition" are used by scientists to talk about thinking; if we don't think about the good things in our life, we would not feel grateful.

Most situations that happen in our lives are neither all good nor all bad. It is on us how we trick our minds and interpret the effect of the situation on our lives. One of the thinking habits is called a "positive interpretation bias," which means that we are most likely to interpret a neutral or negative situation positively. On the contrary, some people tend to ignore all the positive aspects of their problems and finds excuses and reasons to focus more on the negativity.

Studies also show that people who practice gratitude remember more good memories than bad ones. A more grateful person tends to encode more positive memories and keeps out the negative ones. They are also tended to be healthier and are sick less often. This is because they worry less about all the wrong things and focus more on the positive stuff they had achieved throughout the days. They keep their negative emotions to a minimum. A study showed that people who felt more grateful also had increased brain activity essential for both emotional and cognitive processes.

Happiness and gratitude go hand in hand and can be practiced in a lot of different ways. One way is to write a list of all the good things that have happened to you every day and go through it before you sleep. Another way is to send some love to your close ones, thanking and appreciating all that they have done for you. While it is essential to practice gratitude every day, it is also important to know that the bad things shouldn't be ignored. In fact, the real test of gratitude is how we act on the situations when they don't go as per our plans. We don't always need to be happy to be grateful, but gratitude indeed leads to greater happiness.

Chapter 30:
Being Open To Opportunities For Social Events

As we continue from the previous video, something I learned is that things never turn out as how you would expect to in life. And the more we try to force something, the more resistance we face. And the more we take things in stride and just trust the process, the more things tend to flow naturally. You will see what I mean as we go through this video together.

As I was describing about how my social life was basically non existent at one point, if you guys haven't watched that video, do check it out first.

After taking a hard look at the decisions I made that left me with little to no social support or events to go to, i knew that I needed to do a 180 if i hoped to see any sort of rebound in my social life. And I started making a concrete plan with specific actions that would put me in a favourable position to attract and keep new friends.

At my lowest point, I knew that there was little that I could do to salvage my previous relationships, that I had probably done irreparable harm to them and i needed to start all over again. And that is to Make new friends from scratch. It wasn't so much something that I felt i needed right away, but i knew that in the long run, investing in friendships would bring me much more joy than money ever could especially in the latter years of my life. I knew that money wasn't the end all be all, and that people was the way to go.

Money can be made, but friendships cannot be bought.

I started the goal of dedicating this year and beyond to new friendships and began by signing up for activities that were in line with my interests. As an avid tennis fan and a player of the game, i decided that that was where i would begin. I started joining tennis groups and started playing games with complete strangers. Having also a growing interest in yoga and working out, I also started going for classes with my membership. Whilst i did not really make any real friends right away, I felt that I was already connected in some ways to people with similar interests. And I felt like i was part of a community, that I belonged somewhere. The more i showed up for these activities, the more people kept seeing me around, and the more these people started associated me as being regulars. Soon I was invited by one or two people to join a private game and that in itself became a regular thing. I started seeing these faces weekly for a year and we became friends naturally over the game of tennis. Yoga was a different story as it was more of an individual kind of sport, and people were generally more focused on their own practice on the mat, but it was fine as my interest for yoga faded pretty quickly anyway.

At the gym I started making one or two friends as well. It became natural to chat up with the gym regulars and even the staff, i felt like i looked forward to attending these events not because I wanted to work out, but because I enjoyed the social part and meeting my new friends and striking up random conversations.

For those of you who work in 9-5 jobs, you might not face this same issue as me, as meeting new people and colleagues would be a very simple way to start making new aquaintances that could potentially turn into friends... Seeing that you would meet them every single day whether you liked it or not. But for people who work from home or who are self employed, we do need to make the extra effort to meet new people.

As my pool of friends grew bigger, I started forming my own private tennis group, putting in the extra effort to book the courts day in and out, and inviting them to play. Eventually all my hard work paid off, as people reciprocated by inviting me to their own private outings and dinners. And I started to integrate into their lives and their friends. I had made myself so readily available, not by design, but by choice because at that point I was so ready to say yes to anything it became so natural to prioritise hanging out over just simply working all day and night. My friends saw me as someone they could count on to be there and they had no qualms making me a priority when they wanted to find somebody to hang out with. I reciprocated by making them a priority as well. And the friendship blossomed from there.

For the first time in a long time, I felt truly alive. I felt that my life had a purpose, it had balance, it had work and play, there was yin to my yang, and i looked forward to working as much as I looked forward to hanging out.

I don't know how long this bliss will last, but i know that I had made the right choice. This all happened in 2020, smack in the middle of the pandemic, and yet I made it work because I had given myself every opportunity to succeed.

If this story resonated with you, then i challenge each and everyone of you today to simply decide on a time and place you would like to begin changing the areas of your life that you find lacking. The one thing that I have learned from all this is that it is never tooo late to turn things around. Whether it be financial, emotional, or physical. A firm decision to change is all it takes. And giving it time to grow and blossom is essential to seeing long term success.

Chapter 31:
Being Mentally Strong

Have you ever wondered why your performance in practice versus an actual test is like night and day? Or how you are able to perform so well in a mock situation but just crumble when it comes game time?

It all boils down to our mental strength.

The greatest players in sports all have one thing in common, incredibly strong beliefs in themselves that they can win no matter how difficult the circumstance. Where rivals that have the same playing ability may challenge them, they will always prevail because they know their self-worth and they never once doubt that they will lose even when facing immense external or internal pressure.

Most of us are used to facing pressure from external sources. Whether it be from people around us, online haters, or whoever they may be, that can take a toll on our ability to perform. But the greatest threat is not from those areas... it is from within. The voices in our head telling us that we are not going to win this match, that we are not going to well in this performance, that we should just give up because we are already losing by that much.

It is only when we can crush these voices that we can truly outperform our wildest abilities. Mental strength is something that we can all acquire. We just have to find a way to block out all the negativity and replace them with voices that are encouraging. to believe in ourselves that we can and will overcome any situation that life throws at us.

The next time you notice that doubts start creeping in, you need to snap yourself out of it as quickly as you can, 5 4 3 2 1. Focus on the next point, focus on the next game, focus on the next speech. Don't give yourself the time to think about what went wrong the last time. You are only as good as your present performance, not your past.

I believe that you will achieve wonderful things in life you are able to crush those negative thoughts and enhance your mental strength.

Chapter 32:
The Trick To Focusing

If you've been struggling with procrastinations and distractions, just not being able to do the things you know you should do and purposefully putting them off by mindlessly browsing social media or the web, then today I'm going to share with you one very simple trick that has worked for me in getting myself to focus.

I will not beat around the bush for this. The trick is to sit in silence for a minute with your work laid out in front of you in a quiet place free from noise or distractions. I know it sounds silly, but it has worked time and time again for me whenever I did this and I believe it will work the same for you.

You see our brains are constantly racing with a million thoughts. Thoughts telling us whether we should be doing our work, thoughts telling us that we should turn on the TV instead, thoughts that don't serve any real purpose but to pull us away from our goal of doing the things that matter.

Instead of being a victim of our minds, and going according to its whims and fancies. Quieting down the mind by sitting in complete silence is a good way to engage ourselves in a deeper way. A way that cuts the mind off completely, to plug ourselves out of the automated thoughts that don't serve us, and to realign ourselves with our goals and purpose of working.

To do this effectively, it is best that you turn on the AC to a comfortable temperature, sit on your working chair, lay your work out neatly in front of you, and just sit in silence for a moment. What I found that works a step up is to actually put on my noise cancelling headphones, and I find myself disappear into a clear mind. A mind free from noise, distractions, social media, music, and all the possible ways that it can throw me off my focus.

With no noise whatsoever, you will find yourself at complete peace with the world. Your thoughts about procrastination will get crushed by your feelings of serenity and peace. A feeling that you can do anything if you wanted to right now.

Everytime I turned on music or the TV, thinking I needed it as a distraction, my focus always ends up split. I operate on a much lower level of productivity because my mind is in two places. One listening to the TV or music, and the other on my work. I end up wasting more resources of my brain and end up feeling more tired and fatigued quickly than I normally would.

If that sounds familiar to you, well i have been there and done that too. And I can tell you that it is not a sustainable way to go about doing things in the long run.

The power of silence is immense. It keeps us laser focused on the task in front of us. And we hesitate less on every decision.

The next thing I would need you to do is to actually challenge yourself to be distraction free for as long as possible when you first start engaging in silence. Put all your devices on silent mode, keep it vibration free, and do not let notifications suck you back into the world of distractions. It is the number 1 killer of productivity and focus for all of us.

So if u struggle with focusing, I want you to give it a try right. If you know you are distracted there is no harm right here right now to make a choice to give this a shot.

Take out our noise cancelling earphones, turn the ac on, turn your devices off or to silent, lay your work out in front of you, turn up the lights, sit on your chair, close your eyes for a minute, and watch the magic happen.

Chapter 33:
The Things That Matter

Today we're going to talk about a topic that I am very passionate about. Passionate because it has helped to guide each and every decision that I make on a daily basis. Having this constant reminder of the things that matter will put things in perspective for us - to eliminate the things that are taking up our time for the wrong reasons and to focus on the things that we actually want deep down in our hearts.

With that in mind, let's begin.

How many of you can safely say that you know what truly matters in life? How do you define living a successful and fulfilling life? Is it by having a certain net worth? Is it by living a stress-free life? Is it seeing the world? Is it by serving a defined number of people? Is it by having 10 life-long friends that you can count on? Is it by having a certain number of kids? Or have you not really thought about what you really want out of life yet?

Before we can really gear our actions towards the direction that we want to lead it, we must first know exactly what those specific things we want to achieve are.

The things that matter in my life vary over time as I get older and wiser. When I was young I used to think getting good grades, getting into a good university, and getting a good and stable job was all that really mattered, but I have soon come to realize that family, friends, and having people to hang out with were way more important than simply making money. There was a point in my life that I was so driven by money that I created a huge imbalance in my life by spending 99% of my time on my career. This lopsided drive caused me to neglect friendships, relationships, and soon people associated me with always being too busy for anything. I gradually stopped hanging out with anyone altogether. At first it was okay as I thought "hey, I finally have time to do whatever I want" and I don't have to be disturbed by meetups that would disrupt my workflow. But over time, I felt a gaping hole opening up somewhere deep inside that I could not seem to fill. I suddenly realized that I had successfully isolated myself from any and all relationships. This isolation felt increasingly lonely for me. I felt that I had no one to talk to when I was feeling down, no one to share my struggles with, no one to walk this journey with, and I knew I needed to do something about it. It was only after I started reconnecting with my friends did I truly feel alive again. Having friends brought me more joy than money ever did or could. There's a saying that you can't buy happiness; the same is true for friendships - you can't buy them either. They have to be earned and built with trust and loyalty.

For those of you who are so career focused and money-minded, I share from experience that the destination may not be pretty if you do not have friends or family to share it with. Sure you may afford a penthouse or a Ferrari, but what does it really mean? Sure you have a nice view and a fast ride, but can you share your life with it? When you are old and frail, can your house and car support you physically and emotionally? Don't make the same mistake I did for a good 3 years of my life. It was enough time for me to feel completely alone. No amount of acquiring things could fill that hole no matter how hard I tried. Sure I had the fanciest Apple products, my iPad, iPhone, MacBook, iMac, AirPods, the list goes on. Sure I could "make friends" with these shiny objects by using them everyday. But over time it just reminded me more and more that I had replaced people with gadgets, that I had replaced humans with Siri. It was really really sad honestly.

Having friends that don't judge you or who don't care whether you have money or not, those are the real friends that you know you can count on. And I urge those of you who have neglected this big part to start reconnecting old friends or finding new ones altogether who share the same interests as you. Golf buddies, tennis buddies, karaoke buddies, these are good places to start searching for friends and getting the ice broken.

If starting a family is something that you really want in life, have you begun searching for a partner and planning how and when you expect that to happen for you? Sure many of us think we may have a lot of time to do after we get our career going, but how many of us have heard stories of people who just never got off the bandwagon because they've become too busy with their careers? That maybe getting pregnant just never seems like the right time because you don't want to jeopardize your job. Or maybe that you never even got around to dating at all by the time you are 35 because you've become too busy being a general manager of your company. If having a career is the most important thing to you, then by all means go full steam ahead to achieve that goal. However if family is something of great significance to you, you may want to consider starting that timeline right now instead of waiting. Remember the goal is to focus on the things that truly matter. If having a loving spouse who you can grow old with and having say 2 kids who can support you when you are old is what you really want, maybe waiting isn't such a good idea. Finding love takes practice. You will meet frogs along the way and it takes time to grow a lasting relationship. Sure you can rush a marriage if time is of the essence, but is that ideal? Personally I believe a strong relationship takes 2-3 years to build. Do you have that type of runway to play with? Don't work yourself to death at your job only to find yourself rich and alone. Regret will come after for sure.

Whatever else you have defined as the things that matter to you, make sure that you never neglect those priorities. Sometimes life gets so busy and hectic that we forget to stop and refresh ourselves on what we really want to get out of life. It is all too easy for us to operate on autopilot - To set an alarm, go to work, gym, go home, take dinner, sleep, and repeat the day all over again. For weekends, we may be so exhausted from work that we just end up sleeping or wasting our weekend away only to begin the same routine again on Monday.

There's plenty of time for work decades down the road, but dating relationships and friendships may not have that runway of time.

So I challenge each and everyone of you to clearly define what the things that matter mean to you and to take consistent action in these areas day in and out until you can safely say you've already checked them off your bucket list.

Chapter 34:

Keep Working When You're Just Not Feeling It

How many times in a day do you feel like doing nothing? How many times have you had the feeling of getting exhausted and have no energy or motivation to do anything? Do you want answers to these problems? Let's analyze some things.

What were the last big achievement that made you, your family, and your friends proud? When was the last time you had this urge to do a little more work just for the sake of it? Did you feel sorry for yourself and thought how tired you are? These are the problems!

The things that don't make sense to you right now will become more meaningful and purposeful once you get out of your comfort zone. For that, you must start doing what you failed to do the last time.

These feelings of in-activeness and leisure are not a result of some circumstances but the inner voice of every human being that never sleeps and makes us feel like we cannot do this today.

More than often, a change of self is needed than a change of the scenes surrounding us. This is the major task at hand that most people fail to achieve. But we can never give up. This is in fact the spirit of living. The spirit of keep going even when the hardest times hit.

Your body should be the easiest item for you to train and get a hold of. If you are not even able to do that, then there is very little hope for you to achieve anything ever again.

So put yourself in motion and start creating. Instead of thinking about these wrong feelings that your heart gives out just to get you to sleep one more hour, use your time to get creative with life. You don't deserve a good sleep if you haven't done what was meant to be done today. You don't deserve a long breath of relaxation if you haven't tried hard enough to get out of this rut.

You don't feel like getting the job done because you still have a sense of fear and self-pity that keeps you from giving your creative energies another try.

Human beings are the summary of what they repeatedly do, so excellence can also be a habit once you make changes in your behavior for it.

If an inner voice tells you not to do something because you cannot do it, give it a trailer of what is about to come. You will get things done the very first time, and that voice will never bother you again.

These voices and feelings will make you procrastinate rather than performing those actions for real. This is no good way to use your creative energies, just to think of a beautiful scenario and not actually doing something to be in that scenario someday. And laying low because you don't feel like doing it today is the smallest hurdle to pass to get to that place.

All you need is some self-resilience and self-control and the ability to be the master of your body and I doubt there is anything that can stop you then.

Chapter 35:
HOW TO DEVELOP AN INCREDIBLE WORK ETHIC

We've all been there. That feeling of really, really not wanting to go into the office of a morning. It cripples productivity, raises stress levels, and makes us unhappy.

Why Do We Do It To Ourselves?

Unless it stems from deeper issues, the feeling of not wanting to go to work is often the result of a poor work ethic. If you've experienced it yourself recently, that doesn't make you a bad person or employee. A poor work ethic usually arrives subconsciously and is something you'll have little control over or forewarning of its impending arrival.

Thankfully, there are some methods you can employ to improve your work ethic dramatically, and they're not quite as tricky as you might think. To help you get out of that rut and back, fighting fit for a productive time in the office, we've decided to list our top eight tips for improving your work ethic.

1. Start With Your Body – Treat It Right

A healthy body will help you build a healthy approach to work because the two are intrinsically linked.

If you feel lethargic in the morning, the last thing you're going to want to do is to spring out of bed and head to the office. You're far more likely to continually hit the 'snooze' button and curse the fact you even have a job.

Lethargy can be a result of not enough sleep and poor levels of exercise. Therefore if the feeling just described is something you're all too familiar with, it's time to go on something of a permanent health kick. And that doesn't mean ditching all the treats that make you happy – just the process of regularly exercising and eating more healthily.

Walk when you'd normally take the car and swap those regular naughty treats for fruit and glasses of water – you'll be surprised how much more up for it you'll feel each morning.

2. Eliminate As Many Distractions As Possible

How many times do you check your email each day? What about social media? Is your facebook feed something you access every five minutes to check in on what your friends and family are up to?

We live in a world full of distractions. Multiple forms of content, relentless notifications and devices capable of connecting us immediately to the internet are everywhere and seemingly impossible to drag yourself away from.

That's true – unless you can call on your reserves of willpower. Distractions will divert your attention from what matters, and ensure that you have a limited focus on work tasks. In turn, that'll reduce your emotional connection with the business and negatively impact your work ethic.

Check your email only two or three times a day, turn off notifications and leave social media for the moments when you're sat on the sofa with nothing better to do.

3. Measure Your Ethic Against Others

If you're forever cursing your colleague's ability to practically skip into work ready for the day ahead, why not measure your performance against theirs?

Something is different. It might be their mindset, attitude towards their role or lifestyle, but if you can be brave enough to measure your performance against others, you'll quickly suss out where you need to improve.

This can extend far beyond work colleagues, too. For example, if your partner appears to be having the time of their life at work, yet you can barely muster the strength to log onto your computer for the first time each morning, ask them how they're doing it. You never know – you might just learn a thing or two.

Unless you're particularly spritely in the morning, it's unlikely that you'll jump out of bed and head to work full of an endless supply of energy. Still, if you follow our tips above, you'll greatly increase your ability to foster a healthy approach to work. Whenever you feel uninspired by your role, but you know it's something more superficial than job dissatisfaction, check that you're doing all you can to improve your work ethic. As we've demonstrated today, it isn't that difficult at all.

Chapter 36:
10 Stress Management Tips

Most students experience significant amounts of stress, and this stress can take a significant toll on health, happiness, and grades. For example, a study found that teens report stress levels similar to that of adults. Stress can affect health-related behaviors like sleep patterns, diet, and exercise as well, taking a larger toll. Given that nearly half of the survey respondents reported completing three hours of homework per night in addition to their full day of school work and extracurriculars, this is understandable.

1. Get Enough Sleep

Students, with their packed schedules, are notorious for missing sleep. Unfortunately, operating in a sleep-deprived state puts you at a distinct disadvantage. You're less productive, you may find it more difficult to learn, and you may even be a hazard behind the wheel. Don't neglect your sleep schedule. Aim to get at least 8 hours a night and take power naps when you need them.

2. Practice Visualization

Using guided imagery to reduce stress is easy and effective. Visualizations can help you calm down, detach from what's stressing you, and turn off your body's stress response. You can also use visualizations to prepare for presentations and score higher on tests by vividly seeing yourself performing just as you'd like to.

3. Exercise Regularly

One of the healthiest ways to blow off steam is to get regular exercise. Students can work exercise into their schedules by doing yoga in the morning, walking or biking to campus, or reviewing for tests with a friend while walking on a treadmill at the gym. Starting now and keeping a regular exercise practice throughout your lifetime can help you live longer and enjoy your life more.

4. Take Calming Breaths

When your body is experiencing a stress response, you're often not thinking as clearly as you could be. A quick way to calm down is to practice breathing exercises. These can be done virtually anywhere to relieve stress in minutes, and are especially effective for reducing anxiety before or even during tests, as well as during other times when stress feels overwhelming.

5. Practice Progressive Muscle Relaxation (PMR)

Another great stress reliever that can be used during tests, before bed, or at other times when stress has you physically wound up is progressive muscle relaxation (PMR). This technique involves tensing and relaxing all muscles until the body is completely relaxed.

With practice, you can learn to release stress from your body in seconds. This can be particularly helpful for students because it can be adapted to help relaxation efforts before sleep for deeper sleep, something students can always use, or even to relax and reverse test-induced panic before or during a test.

6. Listen to Music

A convenient stress reliever that has also shown many cognitive benefits, music can help you to relieve stress and either calm yourself down or stimulate your mind as your situation warrants. Students can harness the benefits of music by playing classical music while studying, playing upbeat music to "wake up" mentally, or relaxing with the help of their favorite slow melodies.

7. Get Organized

Clutter can cause stress, decrease productivity, and even cost you money. Many students live in a cluttered place, and this can have negative effects on grades. One way to reduce the amount of stress that you experience is to keep a minimalist, soothing study area that's free of distractions and clutter.

This can help lower stress levels, save time in finding lost items, and keep roommate relationships more positive. It can also help students gain a positive feeling about their study area, which helps with test prep and encourages more studying. It's worth the effort.

8. Eat a Healthy Diet

You may not realize it, but your diet can either boost your brainpower or sap you of mental energy. A healthy diet can function as both a stress management technique and a study aid. Improving your diet can keep you from experiencing diet-related mood swings, light-headedness, and more.

9. Try Self-Hypnosis

Students often find themselves "getting very sleepy" (like when they pull all-nighters), but—all kidding aside—self-hypnosis can be an effective stress management tool and a powerful productivity tool as well.

With it, you can help yourself release tension from your body and stress from your mind, and plant the seeds of success in your subconscious mind with the power of autosuggestion.

10. Use Positive Thinking and Affirmations

Did you know that optimists actually experience better circumstances, in part, because their way of thinking helps to *create* better circumstances in their lives? It's true! The habit of optimism and positive thinking can bring better health, baetter relationships, and, yes, better grades.

Learn how to train your brain for more positive self-talk and a brighter future with affirmations and other tools for optimism. You can also learn the limitations to affirmations and the caveats of positive thinking so you aren't working against yourself.

www.ingramcontent.com/pod-product-compliance
Lightning Source LLC
Chambersburg PA
CBHW070921080526
44589CB00013B/1392